Baxter
the travelling cat

Baxter
the travelling cat

Anne Forsyth
Illustrated by Sally Holmes

HODDER AND STOUGHTON
LONDON   SYDNEY   AUCKLAND   TORONTO

Also by Anne Forsyth

BAXTER AND THE GOLDEN PAVEMENTS

BAXTER GOES TO SEA

British Library Cataloguing in Publication Data

Forsyth, Anne
    Baxter the travelling cat.—(Hopscotch series)
    I. Title   II. Series
    823'.9'IJ   PZ7.F77/

    ISBN 0-340-26273-7

First published 1981
Third impression 1987

Published by Hodder and Stoughton Children's Books,
a division of Hodder and Stoughton Ltd,
Mill Road, Dunton Green, Sevenoaks, Kent TN13 2YJ

Photoset by Rowland Phototypesetting Ltd,
Bury St Edmunds, Suffolk

Printed in Great Britain by St Edmundsbury Press Ltd,
Bury St Edmunds, Suffolk

Baxter finished his milk and washed his paws. Then he decided it was time to go visiting.

Baxter was a large ginger cat with extra large paws. If you only saw his paws under the door, you would think he was a lion. But the rest of him was just an ordinary cat.

He was called Baxter because that was the name of the owner of the fish and chip shop where Baxter was born – Baxter's Fish and Chip Emporium. An emporium is a very big shop. Mr Baxter didn't really have a very big shop, but he thought that 'Emporium' sounded

5

much grander than 'shop'.

   Baxter (the cat) liked
   fish and chips
   potato crisps (especially bacon-
   flavoured)
   fighting with the cat next door.
   But best of all he liked visiting.
   He visited
   the old lady next door but one
   the children at the school across the
road
   the newspaper shop on the corner.

   On this particular day he set off to

visit the old lady in the house next door
but one.

But on the way he saw a large van.
Two men were lifting furniture into the
van. The people in the house next door
were moving.

They were going to live in Scotland.

Baxter was very curious. He jumped
into the van and settled down into the
largest, most comfortable armchair he
had ever seen.

The men didn't notice Baxter.
They loaded into the van
a bed
a chest of drawers
two tables
a lot of carpets – and all the other
things you take when you move home.

Then at last one of the men said,
'Right! That's it, then. Off we go.' And
they banged the doors and set off to
drive to Scotland.

And Baxter slept and slept.

When they finally stopped they were
near Inverness. Inverness is right in the
north of Scotland.

The men opened the doors of the van,
and took out the bed, the chest of
drawers, the two tables, the carpets, and
all the other things they had put into the
van. Last of all, they came to the
armchair – and there was Baxter.

'Well,' said one of the men. 'It's their
cat. Wanted a lift to his new home.'

But of course Baxter *didn't* belong to

the people who were moving house.
So . . . Baxter jumped down and
wondered where he was.

'Scotland!' he heard one of the men
say. 'Give me London any day. Nothing
but heather and mountains here.'

'Scotland!' said Baxter. 'Well! Well!'
And he twitched his whiskers and said,
'Let's see what Scotland looks like.'

The first house he came to was a nice
little cottage with a bright red geranium
in the window and a lovely view of
Loch Ness. A loch is a very big stretch
of water, like a lake.

He went up to the gate. Something
delicious was cooking on the stove. So
he stamped on his huge lion's paws, up
to the front door.

In the kitchen was an old lady. Baxter miaowed at her. 'Och, you poor starving beast,' said the old lady. 'You'll take something to eat, a wee drop of porridge.'

So she poured out a plate of porridge and topped it with the best cream.

Baxter ate it down to the very last drop, right down to the pattern on the plate which showed flowers and said, 'A present from Oban'.

The old lady smiled. 'You're a nice beast,' she said. 'Pity you can't stay here.'

'Why not?' Baxter wondered.

'Montgomery wouldn't like it a bit,' said the old lady. 'Here he comes.'

The door burst open and a very angry little black terrier rushed in, yapping fiercely.

It didn't sound a bit friendly from where Baxter was sitting. It sounded like . . . 'Grrr . . . get out of here . . . or I'll . . . grrr . . . get you. . . .'
So Baxter jumped down from his comfortable seat. What a pity! He liked porridge and cream, and the old lady was very kind. But the little black dog didn't like cats.

It was time for Baxter to move on.
So . . .
off he went down to the Loch.
He was sitting enjoying the sunshine when he heard, Squelch, squelch.
'Squelch' is a sound, like the sound of someone in wellingtons walking through mud.

He turned round and saw a huge beast covered with scales and with a large hump on its back. He had never seen anything like it before.

'Who are you?' he asked.

The creature said, very huffily, 'I'm the Loch Ness Monster, of course.'

'What's that?' asked Baxter, his eyes large and round.

'Everyone's heard of the Loch Ness Monster,' said the creature, very crossly indeed.

'I haven't,' said Baxter.

'Well,' said the creature, 'I can't think where you've been. Why, in America and India and Nigeria, they've heard of me. Where *have* you been?'

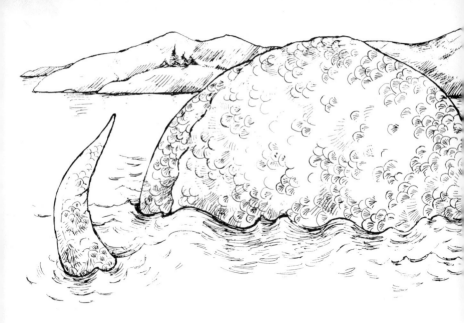

'London,' said Baxter very humbly.

'Huh!' the creature snorted. 'Some people say I'm real and some say there's no such creature, and they come for miles and miles just to get a glimpse of me.'

'Where do you live?' asked Baxter.

'Deep down at the bottom of the Loch.'

'Do you live there all the time?' asked Baxter.

'Yes, except when I come up for a breath of air.'

'And what's down there?'

'Nothing much,' said the Monster.
'Mud and weeds.'

'It sounds a little dull,' said Baxter
timidly.

'Oh, it is,' said the Monster, stamping
its feet. 'You can't believe how dull. I'd
love to go away for a holiday – I believe
it's very pleasant at St Andrews, with
sands and boats and ice creams and all
sorts of things. It sounds so exciting . . .'
and he gave a great sigh and the waters
of the Loch rippled as if a breeze had
passed over.

Suddenly there was the sound of a bus coming round the corner. 'Ah! Visitors!' said the Monster. 'Time I was back at work. Well, it's been nice meeting you, though you are a little stupid. Fancy not knowing about me! But it makes a change to talk to someone besides fish. They always run away. May I shake you by the paw?'

Then, 'Goodbye', said the Monster solemnly, and dived into the deep waters of the Loch.

Just then a coach came round the corner and a lot of people got out, all carrying cameras so that they could take a photograph of the Monster.

But he was right down at the bottom of the Loch.

He didn't come up to the surface at all. He just lay and blew bubbles, so that the visitors looked at the ripples and said to one another, 'Do you think that could be the Monster?'

And the poor Monster sighed again

and thought about the sands at
St Andrews and the boats and ice
creams and all the fun he could have at
the seaside.

It was time for Baxter to move on.
He began to climb the hill above the
Loch. It seemed a long time since he had

enjoyed the porridge at the old lady's cottage. He was hungry.

He came to a little hut with a stove and a pot of soup on the stove.

There was no one near, so Baxter took a good look round – at the wood stacked in one corner, and the extra large boots in the other, and the huge dish on the table.

In the dish lay a very strange creature.

It was
fat
greasy
round

and had a nasty scowl on its face.

It didn't say a word.

Baxter walked carefully round the creature. He put out a paw and patted it – and it rolled off the table out of the door, over the grass.

Baxter sprang but he missed it. It rolled faster and faster.

He flew down the hill after it, fur flying, hissing and spitting.

But the creature rolled on.

At the bottom of the hill, it bumped into a large stone and leapt up in the air. Baxter leapt too, and sank his claws into the creature.

All the fight went out of it. Instead of a stout, roly poly ball, it looked rather sad and very battered.

'That's done for you!' said Baxter proudly.

There was an angry shout and a man with a very red beard came running down the hillside.

'My haggis! That cat's taken it!' he cried. 'My haggis! My dinner!'

Baxter didn't wait to hear more. He ran off as fast as he could. And all the way he could hear the man saying, 'My haggis, my dinner, my haggis – oh, my dinner.'

A haggis is a food you eat in Scotland. It's part of a sheep stuffed with oatmeal and spices. It isn't a real live creature, but Baxter thought it was.

Baxter ran and ran till he came to a
farm. There he crept into the barn and
hid in a great heap of hay.

Suddenly he heard someone coming.
He peeped out and there was a large
black and white cat looking at him.
'What are you doing here?'

'I'm visiting,' said Baxter.

'I can see that,' said the black and
white cat. 'But where do you come
from?'

The strange cat looked friendly, so
Baxter told him the whole story.

'And where are you going now?'
asked the black and white cat.

'I don't know,' said Baxter.

'Tell you what,' said the black and
white cat. 'Come home with me. I live

in a castle. A real castle. With a real live
ghost.'

'Oh.' Baxter blinked. Then he said,
'All right.'

So he followed the black and white
cat into the kitchen of the castle. People
were hurrying backwards and forwards
with plates, and when the cook saw the
two cats, she said, 'Get these cats out of
here!'

But the assistant cook was a kind girl,
and she gave the cats a large plate of
turkey
pieces of chicken
bits of meat
and a large bowl of milk to follow.

The two cats ate and ate, then lay
down to sleep.

When Baxter woke, everything was dark and quiet.

So . . . he decided to look round.

He trotted up the grand staircase. At the head of the staircase was a long corridor.

He tiptoed along the corridor and was just at the corner when he heard a sound that made his fur stand on end.

'Mi.......oooo....aaa..ooooo.uuuuuwww.

He stood very still.

Then round the corner came the ghost of a pure white cat with china blue eyes. It stepped daintily towards Baxter.

He didn't waste any time but turned and ran.

Down in the kitchen the black and white cat lay in front of the fire.

'What's the matter? Seen a ghost?'

'I certainly have,' said Baxter. 'I . . . er . . . think I'll be off now.'

'Please yourself,' said the black and white cat, stretching a lazy paw.

Was it a real ghost? Or was it just a white cat? Well, Baxter thought it was a ghost, but of course he'd had turkey and chicken and scraps of meat and a big bowl of milk.

All next day Baxter walked across the moors. He walked over the heather till he found himself in a little clearing. Late in the afternoon, he curled up under a bush and went to sleep.

What Baxter didn't know was that a troop of Scouts were camping nearby. For two weeks they had slept in tents, cooked their meals out of doors, and explored the country. The Scouts were walking over the moor when all of a sudden one of the boys stopped.

'Look! Tracks! Paw marks!'

All the boys stopped.

'It could be a puma,' said one.

'Or a panther,' said another.

'Escaped from a zoo.'

'Don't be silly – there aren't any zoos near here.'

'Then it must be wild.'

'And dangerous.'

They all peered closely at the tracks in the soft ground leading to the clearing.

'It's got very large paws,' said one.

'It must be a mountain wild cat.'

'Let's find it.'

'Careful,' said the patrol leader. 'It might be dangerous. I'll go first.'

Of course the dangerous animal was

really Baxter. But the boys didn't know
that. Well, you wouldn't expect to find
an ordinary cat in the wild countryside
in Scotland. And Baxter had very large
paws, so it wasn't surprising they
thought it might be a wild beast.

So the leader led the way and the
boys crept after him.

'Sh . . .' said the leader. 'The tracks
have come to an end.' And he took out
a rope he carried with him, just in case
they had to tie the animal up. 'He's at
the back of the·bushes somewhere.'

So they all followed, very quietly, and
what did they see but . . .

Baxter, sound asleep.

'Well,' said the second boy, who really wanted to be leader. 'A panther, you said. A puma. A dangerous wild animal. And all the time it's just an ordinary cat.'

At this Baxter woke up and stretched. 'I'm not an ordinary cat,' he thought rather crossly.

'Come back to camp with us,' said the leader. 'He can share our supper, can't he?' The Scouts were having a special supper because it was the last night of the camp.

Just then, the smallest boy in the troop said,

'See what I've found!'

He'd found a secret place full of wild raspberries.

The Scouts cheered and someone took off his rucksack and someone else found a paper bag, and before long they'd gathered enough raspberries for their supper.

'The cat *must* come back with us,' said the youngest boy. 'He can be our mascot.'

A mascot is something that brings you luck. The boys were lucky because they'd found the raspberries.

So they all marched back to the camp.

'Tonight,' said the leader, 'we cook all the food that's left. So there's sure to be something he likes.'

They cooked
bacon
eggs
sausages
baked beans
and for pudding they had the raspberries. The farmer nearby had sent over a jug of cream because the boys had helped him to rescue a sheep that had strayed on to the road.

34

Baxter lapped up his share of the cream. Then the boys sat round the camp fire and sang and told stories. And they told Baxter he was a very good mascot and could come to camp with them any time he liked.

Next morning Baxter set off again.

He was walking along the road when he met a family of

mother

father

three children

in a car with a trailer on the back.

The children were sad because it was the end of the holiday.

They were going back to Edinburgh to school, going back to

wearing socks and shoes

and sitting at desks

and doing homework

instead of

fishing

boating

and gathering shells.

Baxter decided he would travel with them. So he leapt into the trailer with all the family luggage and fishing rods.

The children sang songs all the way because they were very sad. It was the end of the holiday.

When they got to Edinburgh, Baxter
jumped out of the trailer.

He didn't want to go with them,
because *he* didn't want to go to school.

He was still on holiday and he wanted
to see Edinburgh Castle and the famous
street – Princes Street – and the pipers.

So he strolled along Princes Street
enjoying the sunshine, until he heard a
sound that went 'Wheeehh . . .'

Baxter nearly jumped out of his fur.
'What's that?'

'It's the pipers,' he heard someone
say.

And there they were.

The pipers marched along the street, puffing out their cheeks and blowing their bagpipes.

Leading them was the pipe major. He was twirling his mace – that's a very long silver stick – and he looked very grand.

He twirled it once, twice, three times, and then threw it up in the air.

Baxter thought it was splendid. He lifted his head and joined in the music with a yowl.

The pipe major turned round in surprise.

'Oh, look!'

'What a shame!'

'He's dropped it!'

The whole band came to a stop.

Crash!

Bang!

Whoom!

The pipe major picked up the mace. His face was bright red. He walked towards Baxter and his face got even redder.

'You . . . wee . . .' he shouted.

Baxter dived between the legs of the crowd and ran and ran.

There was a strong breeze blowing, and as Baxter ran towards the end of Princes Street it blew and blew and blew

him right down the steep steps that led to the station.

It blew him right on to the platform where the train for London was waiting.

'All aboard for London.'

'The London train is about to leave.'

Baxter jumped on to the train and found a compartment empty but for an old gentleman who was asleep in one corner. Baxter curled up in the other corner.

'Tickets, please.'

The old gentleman woke up suddenly. 'Dear me, are we in London?'

'Berwick-upon-Tweed, sir,' said the ticket collector. 'And what's this animal doing here? Is he yours, sir?'

The old gentleman blinked. 'No, I've never seen him before.'

'He'll have to go in the guard's van,' said the ticket collector.

'No, no,' said the old gentleman, who had a very kind heart. 'Let him stay here. I'll pay his fare.'

So the ticket collector wrote out a ticket and marked it CAT in big letters.

'Well, I don't know where you've come from,' said the old gentleman to Baxter when the ticket collector had gone, 'but I'm sure you must be hungry.'

And he opened his suitcase and brought out a packet of salmon sandwiches, which he shared with Baxter. Baxter purred his thanks and ate up every bit.

When they got to London, the old

gentleman said, 'Someone in Edinburgh or London, in Scotland or England, has lost a valuable animal. We must find out where you belong.'

So he took Baxter to the nearest police station. 'Please see if you have any reports of a lost cat,' he asked the policeman on duty.

'Mmmm . . . let's see,' said the policeman, looking at a list. 'Diamond ring, ruby necklace, wallet, purse . . . wait a minute. "Reward offered. Ginger

cat. Handsome, clever, has extra large paws. Likes travelling."'

They both looked at Baxter who tried to appear handsome and clever.

'He certainly has very large paws,' said the policeman. 'The largest I've ever seen.'

'This must be the lost cat,' said the old gentleman. 'I'm sure you have quite enough to do, constable, with burglars and other villains, so I will take him home. It's quite near where I live.'

Baxter's house looked just the same.
They'd replaced the flower pot he had
broken, but nothing else had changed.

'I have come to return your cat,
Madam,' said the old gentleman, when

Baxter's owner, Mrs Carr, came to the door.

'Baxter!' she cried. 'I thought you'd gone for good. And here you are, safe and sound. I can't thank you enough,' she said to the old gentleman.

She called to the children and shook the old gentleman by the hand and patted Baxter on the head all at the same time.

The old gentleman wouldn't take the reward. 'Spend it on a special treat for the children – and your splendid cat,' he said.

Later that evening, Mrs Carr said to Baxter, 'I wonder where you've been?'

'If you only knew,' thought Baxter. 'I've been to Scotland, and met the Loch Ness Monster and fought with a haggis – and won, and seen a real ghost in a real castle, and seen the pipers in Edinburgh . . . but no one would believe me.

'Tomorrow,' he said to himself, as he twitched his whiskers and settled down to sleep, 'I'll go visiting again. But this time I'll only go as far as the old lady – next door but one.'